Lloyd was a little black cat with ratty hair that stu

He wasn't fancy like the fluffy cats or graceful like t̶h̶e̶ ̶s̶l̶e̶e̶k̶ ̶o̶n̶e̶s̶.̶ ̶B̶u̶t̶ ̶L̶l̶o̶y̶d̶ ̶d̶i̶d̶n̶'̶t̶ mind — he knew exactly who he was.

"I'm Lloyd the Lion!" he would say proudly.

The other animals weren't quite so sure…

One morning, Lloyd stood in the middle of the park, chest puffed out and tail curled proudly around his paws.

"I'll just stand here looking important," he thought. "Lions don't chase attention — they attract it!"

He gave his best serious lion face... but no one seemed to notice. The squirrels kept digging, the birds kept tweeting, and a duck waddled right past him without even a glance.

Lloyd cleared his throat. "AHEM!"
The duck stopped, blinked at him, then burst out laughing so hard it nearly fell in the pond.
Lloyd's fur ruffled. "Weird... I thought lions were supposed to be admired."

Lloyd wandered further down the path until he spotted a goat chewing on someone's laundry.

"What are you?" Lloyd asked, tilting his head.
The goat chomped down on a sock. "I'm a goat. What are you?"
Lloyd puffed out his chest. "I'm Lloyd the Lion!"

The goat snorted so hard a sock flew out of his mouth. "I don't know what you are," the goat laughed, "but you're definitely not a lion!"
Lloyd sighed and kept walking. "That's odd... I thought lions were supposed to be impressive."

Lloyd spotted a red bird singing on a fence.
"What are you?" Lloyd asked.

"I'm a cardinal," the bird chirped. "What are you?"
"I'm Lloyd the Lion!" Lloyd announced proudly.

The bird snorted. "A lion?!" it squawked. "You look like a dust bunny that crawled out from under the couch!"
Lloyd's whiskers drooped. "Hmm... I thought lions were supposed to be respected."

Lloyd trudged along until he spotted a frog sitting on a rock.
"What are you?" Lloyd asked.

"I'm a frog," it croaked. "What are you?"
"I'm Lloyd the Lion!"

The frog blinked. "Nah... you're more like a wet sock with legs."
Lloyd groaned. "Interesting... I thought lions were supposed to be feared."

Lloyd stomped down the path, trying to look like a big elephant.
"What are you?" he asked a rabbit.

The rabbit looked up. "I'm a rabbit. What are you?"
Lloyd puffed his chest. "I'm an elephant!"

The rabbit blinked. "An elephant? With that tail? You're more like a fluffy sofa."
Lloyd sighed. "Great, now I'm a couch."

Lloyd spotted a duck waddling across the grass.
"What are you?" he asked.

"I'm a duck," the duck quacked. "What are you?"
Lloyd shrugged. "I'm an elephant!"

The duck blinked. "An elephant? With that fur? You're more like a feather duster."
Lloyd sighed. "Lovely, now I'm a duster."

Lloyd sat down, scratching his head.

"Maybe I'm not an elephant…" he thought. "Maybe I'm a crocodile!"
He looked around, trying to look tough.

A passing pigeon squawked, "A crocodile? With that fur? You look like a grumpy pillow."
Lloyd groaned. "So, I'm a pillow now-fantastic.

Lloyd strutted confidently, thinking, "I'm a crocodile now, with lots of teeth!"
He came across a chicken pecking the ground.
"What are you?" Lloyd asked.

The chicken stopped, squinted, and said, "I'm a chicken. What are you?"
Lloyd grinned, showing off his "teeth" (mostly just his gums). "I'm a crocodile!"
The chicken clucked. "A crocodile? With that smile? You're more like a toothless handbag."
Lloyd sighed. "Excellent, now I'm a purse."

Lloyd spotted a raccoon standing on the grass.
"What are you?" Lloyd asked.

"I'm a raccoon. What are you?"
"I'm a crocodile!"

The raccoon snorted. "You look like a hairball with legs."
Lloyd groaned. "Oh, lovely. So now I'm a hairball."

Lloyd stumbled upon a snake sunbathing on a rock.
"What are you?" Lloyd asked.

"I'm a snake. What are you?"
Lloyd sighed. "Apparently, I'm a hairball."

The snake hissed, "Well, at least you're not me — I'm basically a noodle with eyes."
"Fair enough," Lloyd said.

Lloyd spotted a deer lying in the grass.
"What are you?" Lloyd asked.

"I'm a deer. What are you?"
"I'm a crocodile," Lloyd said.

The deer smirked. "Sure… and I'm a houseplant."
Lloyd muttered, "So, now I'm a plant."

Lloyd froze when he came face to face with a real crocodile.
"What are you?" Lloyd squeaked.

"I'm a crocodile," the crocodile grinned. "What are you?"
Lloyd gulped. "Uh… I'm a crocodile too?"

The crocodile chuckled. "You? You're more like a fuzzy slipper with eyes."
Lloyd sighed. "Marvelous, now I'm a slipper."

Lloyd sat in the grass, thinking hard.

"If I'm not a lion... and not an elephant... and definitely not a crocodile... then I must be a skunk."

He gave himself a sniff.
"Hmm... could be."

Skunk?

Lloyd spotted a pig standing alone in the field.
"What are you?" Lloyd asked.

"I'm a pig. What are you?"
Lloyd shrugged. "I think I'm a skunk."

The pig chuckled. "Skunk? You look more like a little footstool."
Lloyd sighed. "Guess that makes me a footstool now."

Lloyd spotted a little rat sitting quietly, minding his own business.
"What are you?" Lloyd asked.

"I'm a rat. What are you?"
"I'm a skunk," Lloyd said.

The rat looked him up and down. "You look more like a confused doormat."
Lloyd sighed. "Wonderful, now I'm a doormat."

Lloyd stumbled upon a bear sitting on its rump, staring into space.
"What are you?" Lloyd asked.

"I'm a bear. What are you?"
"I'm a skunk," Lloyd said.

The bear chuckled. "Skunk? You look like a lint ball with legs."
Lloyd groaned. "Terrific, now I'm a lint ball."

Lloyd noticed a tiny ladybug sitting on a leaf.
"What are you?" Lloyd asked.

"I'm a ladybug. What are you?"
"I'm a skunk," Lloyd said.

The ladybug giggled. "Skunk? You look like a dusty pom-pom."
Lloyd sighed. "Fantastic, now I'm a pom-pom."

Lloyd flopped onto the grass.

"If I'm not a lion, or an elephant, or a crocodile, or even a skunk... then what on earth am I?"
He stared at the sky, waiting for an answer.

It didn't say much.

Lloyd sat up.

"I think I might be a cow," he said.
He tried to moo — "MOOOO!"

He grinned. " Nailed it."

Cow?

Lloyd spotted a chipmunk munching on a berry.

"What are you?" Lloyd asked.

"I'm a chipmunk. What are you?"
"I'm a cow," Lloyd said.

The chipmunk smirked. "Cow? You look like a worn-out teddy bear."
Lloyd sighed. "Sweet, now I'm a teddy bear."

Lloyd spotted a penguin waddling by.

"What are you?" Lloyd asked.

"I'm a penguin. What are you?"
"I'm a cow!" Lloyd beamed.

The penguin chuckled. "Cow? You look more like a hairy cactus."
Lloyd sighed. "Perfect, now I'm a cactus."

Lloyd spotted a little boy exploring with binoculars.
He squinted. "What on earth is that thing?"

The boy lowered his binoculars. "I'm a human! What are you?"
Lloyd, still baffled, said, "I'm a cow."

The boy laughed. "A cow? No, you're just a scruffy little cat."

Lloyd sat there blinking.

"A cat? That's it?"

Lloyd flopped under his tree.

"Well," he said, "at least cats don't have to work for a living."

And with that, he took the longest nap of his life.

The End

Manufactured by Amazon.ca
Bolton, ON

44928436R00017